Surfing the Internet Safely

A Guide for Teens and Adults

by

Whitney Hankison, MCP, CCNA

Surfing the Internet Safely
A Guide for Teens and Adults

iUniverse books may be ordered through booksellers or by contacting:

iUniverse
1663 Liberty Drive
Bloomington, IN 47403
www.iuniverse.com
1-800-Authors (1-800-288-4677)

Internet contents change frequently so the results in the exercises for this book may vary from screen captures shown. Because of the dynamic nature of the Internet, any Web addresses or links contained in this book may have changed since publication and may no longer be valid. The views expressed in this work are solely those of the author and do not necessarily reflect the views of the pulisher, and the publisher hereby disclaims any responsibility for them.

ISBN: 978-0-595-52405-1 (pbk)
ISBN: 978-0-595-62459-1 (ebk)

Printed in the United States of America

Cover Artwork created by John McCarthy, used by permission.

Trademark Acknowledgements

Dedications and Acknowledgements

I would like to dedicate this book to my family. Without their love and encouragement this could not have been possible. I thank my husband John for his never ending support and creative abilities and contributions. I thank God for inspiring the creation and development of this book.

Table of Contents

Introduction

This book is dedicated to teens and adults who use the Internet both as a tool and entertainment. It has been written for the primary purpose of helping teens to be efficient in getting their homework done on the computer and to be a guide when venturing into the social side of the Internet. The book's goal is to help with better safety practices while surfing the web. It has the goal of helping Internet users get the information they need in a safe fashion. It is designed to be used along with a computer.

What the Internet is used for

In society today we use the Internet to write email with family members and friends. We also use it for shopping for everyday needs. For teens in school, it is also a tool for doing homework as well as a social networking tool. The Internet should be used to gain access to the wide world of interesting topics to satisfy what teens wonder about as they use their creative imaginations. Teens can access information about animals, history, our government and many other topics.

As teens surf the Internet it is important that they and the people around them are aware of the best ways of finding the information they want. Teens need to know that they need to be careful about what they look at and how to find topics of interest.

<u>Concepts to be covered</u>

This book is meant to be a guide for teens and adults to use to implement ways to safely surf the Internet. It will:

- *Cover the use of an Internet browser on a Microsoft based computer, going into detail about Internet explorer version 7.*
- *Have examples of some topics teens look for and how to best find the information.*
- *Discuss the different search engines and their results.*
- *Show how to get the information from a browser into another program and how to save the information for use later*
- *Discuss printing from the Internet*
- *Discuss shopping on the Internet*
- *Discuss social networking on the Internet*
- *Discuss some aspects of Internet predatorial behaviors*
- *Have exercises in "put it into practice sections" and two projects at the end of the book*
- *Discuss ideas for teens to share with their parents and teachers to help keep them and their computer safe*

Chapter 1 -
A Briefing on the Basics

In this section we will discuss features of Internet browsers. In specific we will work with Internet Explorer and talk about how it works. Other browsers have very similar ways of doing the same things we'll talk about.

Launching the program

On most machines Internet Explorer is a little icon shaped like an 'e'. The Internet Explorer Icon on my machine is pictured below in Figure 1.

(Figure 1)

You can often find this icon in several places. If you click on the start button and then click on programs you'll see the Internet Explorer program icon. Many times the icon will also be on the desktop or in the area by the start button. Any icon that looks similar to the picture and says Internet Explorer underneath it will get you to the Internet.

Once you launch Internet Explorer the screen will have some standard things on it that you see in many programs that are written to run on Windows computers. For the explanation of some of the items please refer to figure 2 as we go through them.

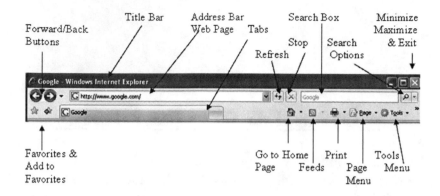

(Figure 2)

We'll explain figure two going from left to right,—— row by row.

In the upper part of the screen you will see what is called a title bar. In most programs, the title bar will tell you the name of the program, and for some browsers it will also list what web page you are on.

To the right of the title bar you have the minimize, maximize and exit buttons. The minimize button takes Internet Explorer off the screen but does not close it. When minimized, Internet Explorer will still show at the bottom of the Windows screen down to the right of the start menu. The maximize button will bring Internet Explorer back up from being minimized. The exit button exits Internet Explorer, closing all of the web pages that are open.

On the next row, on the left you will see the forward and back buttons. They move you between web pages that you have been on. We'll do an exercise with them shortly.

Next to the forward and back buttons is the address bar. This lists the exact location where the browser currently is. This can be a very complicated address if you have gone deep into a web site to search for something.

Next to the address bar are two arrows in a circle. That is the refresh button. You would use this button when you want to see a newly refreshed view of what you're looking at.

Next to the refresh button is the red x, or the stop button. You use this button when you typed something by accident and don't want to wait for it to come up with an error. You can then hit the forward and back buttons to get back where you should be.

Next to the stop button is the search box. You type words in here for the topic that you want to search the Internet on.

Next to the search box is the search options. These options help you choose how you want to search for topics. We'll go over these options in more detail later.

On the final row, the left two icons are for favorites. Here is where you can save your favorite places and get back to them later.

Next to the favorites icons are the tabs for where you are on the internet. You can open many places at the same time. Not all browsers use tabs, some have a different screen for each place where you are. You would look at the bottom of the screen in the row by the start menu to see the different windows that are open.

The next icon looks like a home. This is the icon you push if you want to go to the "home page". The home page is the page that comes up each time you open Internet Explorer program.

The next icon is a feeds icon. This is for getting updates to web sites that host items such as news, blogs or podcasts. An RSS feed is a feed of written material that is summarized and accumulated on a periodic basis so the subscriber can keep up to date on certain material. Podcasts are similar, but in an audio format.

The next icon is a printer that prints everything on the web page you're on.

The next icon is the page menu. It lets you save the page, forward the page by email, change the page or copy the page to another program.

The next icon is the tools menu. It lets you turn off and on a menu, look at other toolbars and choose options to help protect your computer.

Also available in most browsers is a menu bar. The menu bar for Internet Explorer is shown in figure 3 below and has many of the same options on it that other browsers do. Below figure 3 is an outline of the menu and what options are available.

File   Edit   View   Favorites   Tools   Help

(Figure3)

The file menu has options on it to open and close tabs, print options and the exit option to close the program.

The edit menu allows you to copy and paste information. It also lets you select an entire web page. It also helps you with a find option, which allows you to find a particular word on the current web page.

The view menu allows you to bring up more toolbars, and has stop, refresh, back and forward options.

The favorites menu allows you to view, organize and add to your collection of favorite web site links.

The tools menu is similar to the tools option on the toolbar. It lets you turn off and on a menu, look at other toolbars and choose options to help protect your computer.

The help menu allows you to bring up local help, and go on the Internet for help.

Web Site Naming Conventions

Web sites are named a certain way on purpose. There are standards to the way that web sites are named so we can find things easier. All websites are categorized by their ending. A few common ones and their explanations are listed below.

.COM - Commercial - The widest used, many companies that are on the Internet use the .COM extension.

.EDU - Education - primarily 2 and 4 year colleges

.GOV - Government - These are websites that are linked to the Federal Government. An example would be www.whitehouse.gov.

.MIL - Military - Sites linked to Military. Examples would be sites like the Army, Air Force, Navy, or Marines.

.ORG - Organization - These are Sites that are primarily not-for-profit businesses. Sometimes the site may be linked to local Government.

Country Codes - There are websites that have a country code for an ending. The ending is used by some local governments, such as ci.los-angeles.ca.us for the City of Los Angeles, co.los-angeles.ca.us for the County of Los Angeles. Some examples of other country codes are .af for Afghanistan, .uk for United Kingdom, and .th for Thailand.

It is important that we know the correct ending of a website that we are typing. Unfortunately, there are people who put bad things on the Internet on purpose hoping people will mistype the ending of a popular name. If someone gives you a website to type make sure they are giving it to you correctly, you don't want to end up in the wrong place!

Using Search Engines

Search engines are powerful tools that help us find what we want. It is very important when using a search engine to be very specific so we don't end up in a potentially bad web site. There are many search engines, some are new, and some are old. Why are there so many? Each one has a different way to search the web for the information you are looking for. Some specialize in finding certain items, others are more general. In this section I will list a few of the major search engines and we will actually use a very popular search engine to find some interesting things.

All of the listed search engines are safe to go to, give a lot of information about each site listing and look to be around for a long time. Some of the major search engines that qualify are:

Ask.Com - This is a site that actually has an "Ask for kids" section which is especially made to help kids find information for their homework in a safer manner than other search engines. Use this site by typing www.ask.com in the address bar. If you want to go directly to the "Ask for kids" section you would type www.askforkids.com.

Google - A very popular choice, easy to use. This site is a good alternative to Ask.Com when needing a broader search. Use this site by typing www.google.com in the address bar.

Windows Live - Previously Search.MSN.COM this is a Microsoft sponsored search engine. Use this site by typing www.live.com.

AOL - AOL is a popular search engine, especially for people who have AOL based email or belong to AOL as an Internet provider. Use this site by typing search.aol.com in the address bar.

Yahoo - This is very popular as well. It is one of the oldest search engines and does a good job of finding things. Use this site by typing www.yahoo.com in the address bar.

These search engines let you search for images, discussions, news or anything in general. The first site, Ask.Com has the Ask for Kids section which is a very safe way to surf the internet for homework related material. They even have a news section that contains news that kids are interested in!

Let's go back just a minute and look at a certain feature in Internet Explorer again. In Figure 2 we outlined a search box. This search box is set up on the computer to search a particular search engine, and the one it will search will be listed in this box in light type. If you want to change the one that's listed you would click the down arrow in the search options area and choose change search defaults from the menu. On the screen that comes up you can choose a different search engine and click set default to use that one from now on. From search options there is also a menu item to add providers, or add other search engines to the list if the one you are looking for isn't in the list.

Put it into practice:

Now let's put what we just learned into practice. The following is a list of exercises to do to help you find things by using a search engine.

1. *Launch Internet Explorer*
2. *In the Address Bar, type www.ask.com. This brings up the Ask.Com website. On the right side, choose "ask for kids".*
3. *On the right side of the screen click on the Dictionary icon. When the screen comes up type the word Internet in the find box and click find. Read the definition.*
4. *If using Internet explorer, look in the search box to see what search engine you are using. Use the options to look at different search providers you have on your computer, but don't make any changes.*
5. *In the address bar type www.google.com. In the Google search box type "National Zoo". You should find entries listing that talk about the national zoo and giant pandas.*

Using Help

Like most programs, browsers have help. The help is standard Windows help so we will go over some of the features here. By going over them it will also assist you with using help in other programs. You can access help by pressing F1 on the keyboard or choosing help, then contents or index from the menu bar.

We will look at Figure 4 below and discuss the features of help.

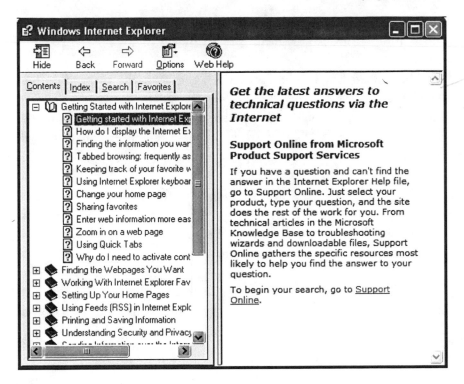

(Figure 4)

In the help screen we have a toolbar across the top, then a tabbed box below that, then the box for the help explanations to the right. In the toolbar across the top we have hide, back, forward, options and web help.

The hide button hides the tabbed box. The button text changes to show when pressed so you can show the tabbed box again.

Back and forward move you around the help screens you've already pulled up.

The option buttons allows you the same options as the other buttons on the tool bar in a menu form, while also providing the choices for stop and refresh.

The web help buttons lists a short cut to be able to search for help on the Internet instead of within the local help files.

The tabbed box is what you will work with the most. The tabs across the top are contents, index, search and favorites. Clicking on items in the tabbed box pulls up the information in the box to the right. The box to the right is where all of the help explanations will come up.

The contents tab lists all of the primary topics that help contains. You can click on these topics to dig deeper into the help of the topic you choose. They are organized into volumes and subtopics so that it guides you to what you want help on.

The Index tab allows you to see an index of words that relate to browsing. This list goes deeper than the contents list and is organized alphabetically. It allows you to type in a 'keyword' to look up in the Index.

The search tab allows a free-form search of the help files for a topic phrased as you choose. You type the word of your choice then click the list topics button to have it list the topics that relate to the word you typed. It is made up from topics and subtopics from the contents tab.

Favorites allow you to go to a previously saved topic, or save the topic you currently have in the help explanations screen.

Put it into practice:

Now let's put what we just learned into practice. The following is a list of exercises to do to help you remember the help options.

1. *Launch Internet Explorer*
2. *Press F1 or choose help, contents and index from the menu bar*

3.   *In the tabbed box, click on Getting started with Internet Explorer*

4.   *In the tabbed box, click on Using Internet Explorer Keyboard Shortcuts*

5.   *In the explanation box there will be the title "Using Internet Explorer Keyboard Shortcuts". Take a minute to read through the tips, you will find them helpful!*

6.   *In the tabbed box click on the index tab.*

7.   *In the keyword box type "shor"*

8.   *Looking in the list underneath, double-click on keyboard shortcuts*

9.   *In the box that pops up choose "Using Internet Explorer Keyboard Shortcuts". You will see that this was another way to bring up the same explanation as before.*

10.   *In the tabbed box, click on the Search tab*

11.   *In the keyword box type "shortcuts" and click on the list topics button*

12.   *Somewhere in the list you will find "Using Internet Explorer Keyboard Shortcuts" again. Double clicking on the topics listed will bring them up in the explanation box.*

Building a favorites list

Browsers have what is called a favorites list. In most browsers this is a list of web sites that you go to the most. You can categorize and organize your favorites so that you can find them easily. In this section we will go through adding to and organizing the favorites using specific examples from Internet Explorer.

For our example we will go to the MSN Encarta site, which is an encyclopedia site that the askforkids.com site uses, and save it in our favorites. You add items to your favorites by first going to the site you want to add. First we need to find the Encarta site. To find the site we'll go to Google and type Encarta in the search box. Since Encarta is such a unique name, the search comes up with the MSN Encarta site with the first listing. By reading the listing we would find that the

MSN Encarta site is Encarta.msn.com. By typing Encarta.msn.com in the address bar we get to the site. We'll examine Figure 5 below to see how we would add it to our favorites.

(Figure 5)

As you can see in figure 5, the Encarta.MSN website is showing and the favorites menu has been clicked on. In the favorites menu you can see you can choose add to favorites. This brings up a box where you can either accept the name of the website, or name it something that you would like better. After you click on the box it will add it to your favorites list. Looking again at figure 5 it would show up right at the bottom after all of the folders.

Another way to add a website to the favorites list is to choose "add to favorites" icon. It is the star icon with the plus in it shown in figure 5 on the left side. The other icon shown on the left side is a plain star. The plain star brings up the favorites center where all of the favorites are listed. By choosing the Favorites Center it allows you a choice to have your favorites on the screen at all times. See figure 6 for a picture and explanation of how that works.

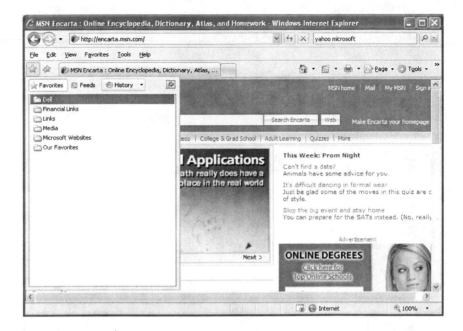

(Figure 6)

As you can see in figure 6 the favorites list is shown. If you click on a folder it shows what the folder has in it. If you look in the Favorites Center box, in the upper right corner you will see an arrow pointing to the left. This allows you to choose to see your favorites list all the time when you are in Internet Explorer. If you make a menu show all the time it is known as "docking" the menu. If you choose the arrow on the favorites screen you will "dock" the favorites screen.

The other thing we want to do with our favorites is organize them so they are easy to find. Looking back at Figure 5, which showed the favorites menu item, you will see an Organize Favorites option on the menu. Looking at Figure 7 below, we will explain what you can do to organize your favorites.

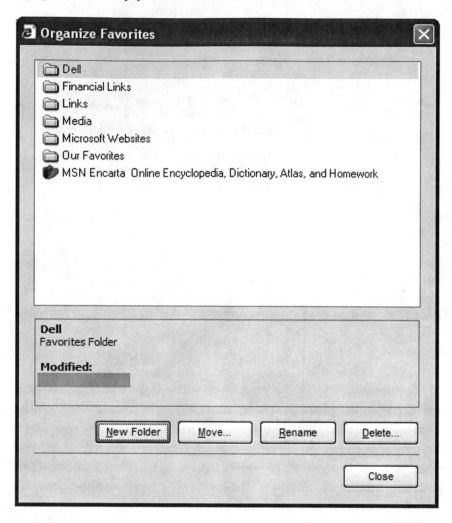

(Figure 7)

Since many people in a home use the computer we want to keep it organized so everyone can find their favorites. To begin to organize our favorites we want to create our own folder to keep them in. You can name folders by subject or you can put your name on a folder, and then organize it by subject under that as well. You create a folder by choosing the New Folder button as shown above in Figure 7. When you click the New Folder button all it asks for is a folder name. Then your new folder shows up in the folder list. To move favorites into your new folders you choose the favorite you want to move, and then choose the Move button. Once you choose the move button you will pick the folder to move it into. Looking once more at Figure 7, you can also delete and rename your favorites from this screen. When you are done, click the close button.

Put it into practice:

Now let's put what we just learned into practice. The following is a list of exercises to do to help you add to and organize your favorites.

1. *Launch Internet Explorer*
2. *In the Address Bar, type Encarta.MSN.com. This brings up the MSN Encarta website.*
3. *Add this to your favorites by choosing the "add to favorites" icon (the star with the plus).*
4. *Bring up the favorites center (click on the star icon)*
5. *Create a folder with your name for a title.*
6. *Move your new MSN Encarta favorite into your new folder.*

Chapter 2 - How to Analyze Search Results

In this chapter we will go over some search examples and their results. We want to be very specific in our searches so that we stay away from bad sites. We will be going through quite a few of the Ask for Kids related sites because they are a good source of information while staying safe.

Staying Safe TIP:

Many places have computers that are for public use. If a computer is in a public place it is very, very likely that it has no safety features meant to help teens stay away from bad sites. These computers should only be used when adult supervision is very close to help when teens are trying to search things out on the Internet. Public Libraries, colleges and Internet café's generally are examples where no teen friendly tools are used because of freedom of speech laws. Of course, each state has different laws so this may vary depending on where you live. It is always best for teens to check with parents, and for parents to check out what tools are on the computers that their children will be using.

More information about tools designed to keep teens safe is discussed in chapter 6.

Examples:

Example 1 - Finding a country and its flag

Finding places is a very important task that the Internet can help with. On the Ask for Kids website there is a World Atlas. After you choose World Atlas, as shown in Figure 8, you can type a country name in the find box and then press the enter button on the keyboard to have it bring up a map of the country you need. Figure 8 shows the results of a search for Brazil, which is in South America.

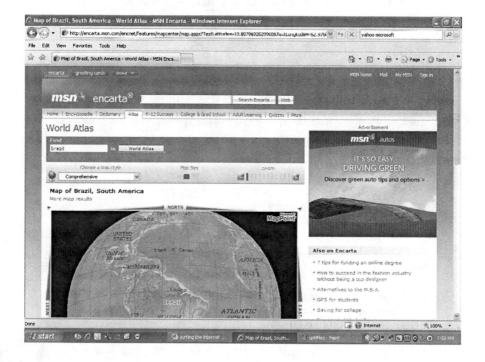

(Figure 8)

If you wanted to go a little farther you can type Brazil in the Ask for Kids search box and they will list all of the important facts about Brazil. Below is a partial list of what comes up when Brazil is searched for:

Background:	Following three centuries under the rule of Portugal, Brazil became an independent nation in 1822 and a republic in 1889. By far the largest and most populous country in South America, Brazil overcame more than half a century of military intervention in the governance of the country when in 1985 the military regime peacefully ceded power to civilian rulers. Brazil continues to pursue industrial and agricultural growth and development of its interior. Exploiting vast natural resources and a large labor pool, it is today South America's leading economic power and a regional leader. Highly unequal income distribution and crime remain pressing problems.
Location:	Eastern South America, bordering the Atlantic Ocean
Geographic coordinates:	10 00 S, 55 00 W
Map references:	South America
Area:	total: 8,511,965 sq km land: 8,456,510 sq km water: 55,455 sq km note: includes Arquipelago de Fernando de Noronha, Atol das Rocas, Ilha da Trindade, Ilhas Martin Vaz, and Penedos de Sao Pedro e Sao Paulo
Area - comparative:	slightly smaller than the US
Land boundaries:	total: 16,885 km border countries: Argentina 1,261 km, Bolivia 3,423 km, Colombia 1,644 km, French Guiana 730 km, Guyana 1,606 km, Paraguay 1,365 km, Peru 2,995 km, Suriname 593 km, Uruguay 1,068 km, Venezuela 2,200 km
Coastline:	7,491 km
Maritime claims:	territorial sea: 12 nm contiguous zone: 24 nm exclusive economic zone: 200 nm continental shelf: 200 nm or to edge of the continental margin
Climate:	mostly tropical, but temperate in south
Terrain:	mostly flat to rolling lowlands in north; some plains, hills, mountains, and narrow coastal belt
Elevation extremes:	lowest point: Atlantic Ocean 0 m highest point: Pico da Neblina 3,014 m
Natural resources:	bauxite, gold, iron ore, manganese, nickel, phosphates, platinum, tin, uranium, petroleum, hydropower, timber
Land use:	arable land: 6.93% permanent crops: 0.89% other: 92.18% (2005)
Irrigated land:	29,200 sq km (2003)
Total renewable water resources:	8,233 cu km (2000)
Freshwater withdrawal (domestic/industrial/agricultural):	total: 59.3 cu km/yr (20%/18%/62%) per capita: 318 cu m/yr (2000)
Natural hazards:	recurring droughts in northeast; floods and occasional frost in south
Environment - current issues:	deforestation in Amazon Basin destroys the habitat and endangers a multitude of plant and animal species indigenous to the area; there is a lucrative illegal wildlife trade; air and water pollution in Rio de Janeiro, Sao Paulo, and several other large cities; land degradation and water pollution caused by improper mining activities; wetland degradation; severe oil spills

	party to: Antarctic-Environmental Protocol, Antarctic-Marine Living Resources, Antarctic Seals, Antarctic Treaty, Biodiversity, Climate Change, Climate Change-Kyoto Protocol, Desertification, Endangered Species, Environmental Modification, Hazardous Wastes, Law of the Sea, Marine Dumping, Ozone Layer Protection, Ship Pollution, Tropical Timber 83, Tropical
Environment - international agreements:	Timber 94, Wetlands, Whaling signed, but not ratified: none of the selected agreements
Geography - note:	largest country in South America; shares common boundaries with every South American country except Chile and Ecuador

This lists some pretty interesting facts! At this point we might be looking for something specific about Brazil, perhaps what the country's flag looks like. In that case we could turn to the Google search engine and find out what the flag looks like. In the Google search box we would type something as specific as possible, such as "Brazil country flag". See figure 9 below for the top 5 results of the search on Google.

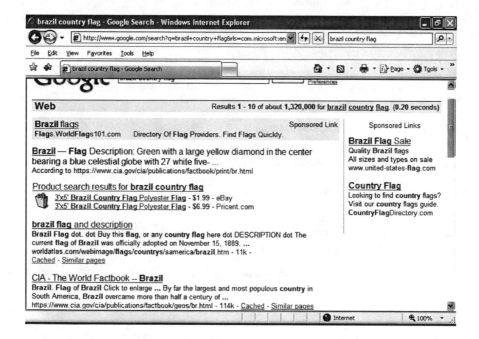

(Figure 9)

There are a couple of really good lessons found in the listing in Figure 9. When you search a general search engine like Google, many times you will get a mix of results. There can be sites to buy things that look like what you searched on. It might list sites that simply contain the word you searched on, but not quite what you are looking for. Somewhere in the list there should be a site that you can get to what you are looking for. I can't repeat enough to be specific in your searches and be careful to read all of the results before clicking on any. When you find a listing that sounds like what you are looking for you want to read the website address found at the bottom of the listing to confirm that it sounds like a good place to go for your information.

Let's take a good look at the results listed in Figure 9.

- *The first listing is for a flag provider - this means a place that sells flags. Unless we want to buy a flag this is not going to be a site that will help us.*
- *The second listing - "Brazil - flag Description" is sounding better so we want to look at the bottom line of the listing for what the website address is. You can often tell what type of website it is by the name of it. The name is "https://www.cia.gov/.... ", a .gov address so we know that it is a government sponsored web page, and very likely to be safe.*
- *The third listing - "Product search results for Brazil Country Flag" is another sales related site. If you ever see eBay as part of a search result it is a sales related site.*
- *The fourth listing - "Brazil Flag and Description" sounds like it would be just what we're looking for. Looking at the website listed at the bottom we can see it says "worldatlas.com/webimage/flags...." so it is the worldatlas.com website. This is a good, comprehensive website but sometimes has some inappropriate ads on it for younger teens, so parents should be asked before using it.*
- *The Fifth listing - "CIA - World Fact Book - Brazil" sounds pretty safe. Looking at the website listed at the bottom it is a repeat site from one of our first results, "https://www.cia.gov/cia/publications", and we can see again that it is a government sponsored site, so is probably safe.*

By looking at the last site on our list, we see it is the listing that was closest to what we were looking for. It seems to be safe, and yes, we will find the picture of the Brazil flag.

Example 2 - Finding some history about the United States

Finding Information about the history of the United States we live in is something each middle and high school student will do from time to time. Let's start by using the askforkids.com website and typing in United States History into the search box. Below is Figure 10 showing our results.

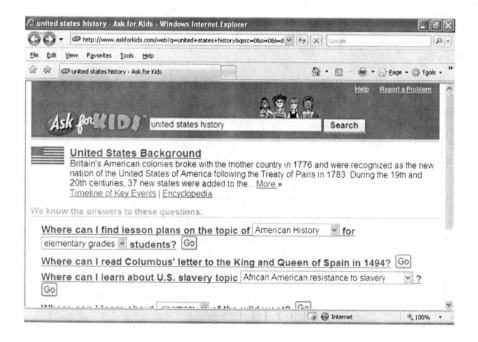

(Figure 10)

I want to take a moment to point out that on this askforkids.com results page there are very valuable result tools. If you look in figure 10 there is a drop down box by multiple phrases. These drop downs list several topics of information. So while this page is rather specific and not for another country, there is great detail here for the United States. At this point we could hit the go button to the right of any of the topic boxes to go to a listing that shows a good deal of history for the United States in a safe manner.

Let's now use Google and do a similar search and look at the results. We'll type "United States history" in the Google search box and look at the results below in Figure 11.

(Figure 11)

Let's take a good look at the results listed in Figure 11.

> The first listing is simply titled "United States History. Let's look next at the web site listed at the bottom of the listing. It says "www.billofrightsinstitute.org". This is a not for profit group sponsored page, which is usually safe, so this looks like a promising listing.
>
> The second listing is "News Results for United States History", which is interesting because it actually lists further links for our topic. The first one doesn't look promising because it talks about a current movie, which isn't exactly what we were looking for. The second talks

about *"Today in History - Nov 2"*, *which could be interesting if we were looking for past events for a certain date. As we look at the bottom of this particular listing we find one that says "American History Series: A clash of cultures in the new world" and we will notice that it is sponsored by Voice of America which is an old and responsible news agency.*

• *The last listing is "History of the United States - Wikipedia, the free encyclopedia". It is very common to come upon Wikipedia entries. There are mixed reviews regarding the information found in Wikipedia, and some information is definitely not meant for youth age people to be reading.*

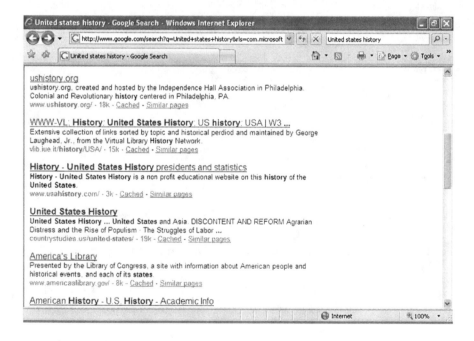

(Figure 12)

To continue our analysis, we'll look at the next few listings as shown in Figure 12.

· *The first listing shown in Figure 12 is "USHistory. ORG". This listing looks rather promising as it says it is created and hosted by the Independence Hall association in Philadelphia. That should be a great place to find out anything specific to our Independence and the events surrounding that period of time.*

· *The next listing is "www-vl:History:United States History: US History etc...." This is an interesting listing to analyze, as it is listed as being maintained by a particular person. Safety Tip: Although these types of listings can be perfectly safe, if there are other good listings it's best to stay away from them until they can be checked by an adult. In this case the listing is fine, but you can never be too cautious!*

· *The next listing is "History - United States History presidents and statistics". This looks promising if presidents and statistics are what we are after. The listing says it is sponsored by a non-profit organization, however the web site listing at the bottom ends in .com. Safety Tip: If listed, the sponsored organization should really match the ending of the website. In this case the web site is really a link to an advertising and search engine ad site, so it's best to avoid these combinations!*

· *The next listing is listed simply as "United States History". The description makes it sound like it is a valid site listing history of the United States and also mentions Asia. By looking at the website at the bottom of this particular listing we can see that it is an .us ending which oftentimes is a government sponsored page. In fact this page has listed on it that the information was received from the US Department of State, so that lends credibility to it being a good site for the information we're looking for.*

· *The last listing we'll look at is titled "America's Library" and says it's presented by the Library of Congress. All published books are registered with the Library of Congress so this could potentially be a great source of*

> *information. Before we act too quickly however, let's examine the website address at the bottom of the listing. Sure enough it says its www.americaslibrary.gov, a government sponsored link, so this should be safe.*

I would say, depending on the exact information you were looking for, the best site from the above list would be the first listing if we were looking for the most information we could find regarding United States History from our short list of results that we analyzed. The last entry looked very promising as well. The lesson learned from our analysis is to be wary of links sponsored by individuals or ending in .com because you're not always sure where they'll lead.

Put it into practice - Item 1:

Now let's put what we just learned into practice. The following is a list of exercises to do to help you find things on AskforKids.com and Google.com.

1. *Launch Internet Explorer*
2. *In the Address Bar, type www.ask.com. This brings up the Ask.Com website. On the right side, choose "ask for kids".*
3. *In the search box type in "United States Government".*
4. *On the results screen click the GO button and it will take you to where you can get more listings regarding our government.*
5. *In the address bar type www.google.com. In the Google search box type the same thing that you did in the askforkids.com search box. You should find entries listing that talk about your our government.*

In this chapter we went through a couple of examples of items youth today need to use for school homework. It is important to practice the skill with an adult present so I've included one more exercise in this chapter for an adult to help the readers with.

Put it into practice - Item 2:

Now let's put what we just learned into practice one more time! The following is a list of exercises to do to help you find more things on AskforKids.com and Google.com.

1.   *Launch Internet Explorer*
2.   *In the Address Bar, type www.askforkids.com.*
3.   *In the search type the name of your favorite animal.*
4.   *On the results screen click the GO button and it will take you to where you can read about your favorite animal.*
5.   *In the address bar type www.google.com. In the Google search box type the same thing that you did in the askforkids.com search box. You should find entries listing that talk about your favorite animal. Go over this list with an adult and discuss which entries will give you the most information.*

Chapter 3 - Working with Information you Find

It is very useful if we can use the information we find on the Internet. We can use it for homework, to impress our family, or just for fun. We can copy this information into a word processing or graphics program to use in a report, or we can print the information on a printer. Tip: It is important that if you use information you find on the Internet that you give credit to the place you got it from. See a teacher for the specific ways they want you to show that you are including information from the Internet in your homework.

For our example we will take a look at the subject of whales from the MSN Encarta website. To get to the MSN Encarta Site we type Encarta.MSN.Com on the address bar. On the Encarta site, there is a search box near the top of the page. In the search box we will type whales. This lists several topics on whales, and for this example we'll pick the listing whose title is "Blue Whale, the largest living animal."

Looking at different views of Internet content

When you wish to do more than read what you find on the Internet it is helpful to know a little about different views you can choose to see the information. For instance, on our Encarta results about whales there are a few options we should go over. See Figure 13 below for our results screen.

Related Items
- Whales, giant marine mammals
- *see also* Endangered Species

more...

Encarta Search

Search Encarta about **Blue Whale**

Give us feedback

View recently updated articles

Blue Whale

Encyclopedia Article

Find | Print | E-mail | Blog It

Multimedia

2 items

Blue Whale, largest <u>whale</u>, and the largest living creature on Earth. Blue whales are found in all oceans of the world. Most populations migrate extensively, traveling from the Tropics or near Tropics in winter to the edges of the pack ice in the northern and

(Figure 13)

On the screen in figure 13 we have text, a picture, and some choices above the article too. It is the choices we want to look at first. Along the top of the picture there is a find and a print option. On different web sites these may say preview, printer friendly view, editable view or similar words may be used. Basically these other views make the article easier to print and work with. This article is a very busy page with ads and other things that would make it hard to work directly with the information or print it so let's look at the results of using the buttons. We'll choose the find button, and see the results in Figure 14 below.

To find a specific word, name, or topic in this article, select the option in your Web browser for finding within the page. In Internet Explorer, this option is under the **Edit** menu.

The search seeks the **exact word or phrase** that you type, so if you don't find your choice, try searching for a key word in your topic or recheck the spelling of a word or name.

Blue Whale

Blue Whale, largest whale, and the largest living creature on Earth. Blue whales are found in all oceans of the world. Most populations migrate extensively, traveling from the Tropics or near Tropics in winter to the edges of the pack ice in the northern and southern hemispheres in summer. Blue whales produce loud, low-frequenc moans that travel over thousands of kilometers underwater. It is likely that they communicate by means of these moans, enabling the members of a group to remain in contact across a vast expanse of ocean.

(Figure 14)

As you can see in Figure 14 the article is easier to read and looks more like a book format. This format prints well and allows you to select text to work with. If we had chosen the print button there would be a print option on the screen instead of the "search view" words. The other options listed in Figure 13 were email, and Blog It. If you are familiar with Email on your computer, you can choose this to send a friend the article you pulled up. Blogging is a method to discuss topics on the Internet with others. Since you never know who the others really are, I would recommend that the Blog It choice should be only done when working with a parent or teacher for additional guidance. It's important to apply safety rules when you are on the Internet such as not talking to strangers. Get parental guidance on the blogging sites that are teen friendly and safe.

Selecting parts of the screen to work with

Once you pull up a good view of an article to work with you can do many things with it. One of the most common things you will want to do is select a piece of text to either print or work with in another program. Selecting text can be a little tricky and requires a lot of patience and practice. The common term used when you select text is that you highlight it. To highlight text, you will hold down the left mouse button and move the mouse over the text you want to select. It is easiest to start from the left and move to the right. If you want to highlight multiple lines you will move the mouse down and to the right. If you want to highlight text that is more than the current screen it is sometimes easiest to use the keyboard to help you. To highlight text with the keyboard, you will start by pointing with the mouse to the place you want to start and highlighting the first word. You can then go to where you want the highlight to end and hold down the Shift Key and click with the left mouse button. The highlight should then include everything between the first word and where you ended.

Put it into practice:

Now let's put what we just learned into practice. The following is a list of exercises to do to help you highlight words with the mouse.

1. *Launch Internet Explorer*
2. *In the Address Bar, type Encarta.MSN.com. This brings up the MSN Encarta website.*
3. *In the Encarta search box type whale*
4. *Pull up the topic on Blue whales*
5. *Click on the find option*
6. *With the mouse, in the first sentence highlight the word Blue*
7. *With the mouse again, in the third sentence highlight the words "Blue whales produce".*
8. *With the mouse once more, we want to highlight the first paragraph with a little help from the keyboard. First, go back and highlight the first word of the paragraph, which was the word Blue. Now go to the last word of the paragraph, ocean, and while holding down the shift key on the keyboard, click with the left mouse button just after the word ocean. This should have highlighted the entire paragraph.*

A little more about Printing

As I mentioned earlier, printing can be a little tricky. Many web pages will get cut off on the right side of the paper. You always want to look for a print or printer friendly icon on the web page to make sure that it prints correctly.

In addition to printing the whole article, you can choose to print just a part or print multiple copies. By choosing the File option from the Menu on most browsers you will be able to choose print. We'll use Figure 15 to go over all of the options on the Print screen.

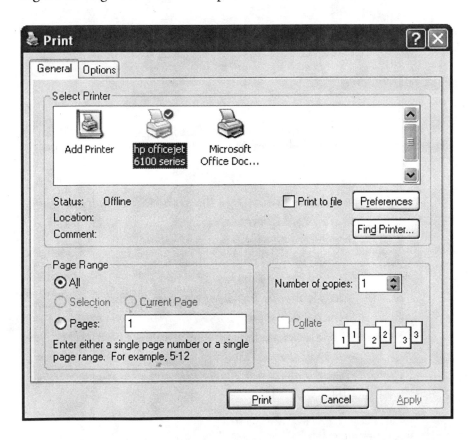

(Figure 15)

As you can see in figure 15 the page range box has many choices. If you want to print the whole page you can simply click on print. If you want to print certain pages, say pages 1 and 2 you can type "1-2" in the pages box. Many times you will want to print just a portion of the web page or just certain pages of an article you've pulled up. If you want to print just a section you would first want to use the mouse to highlight that portion of the article. Then when you choose File, Print from the menu, you would click on selection to print the area you highlighted. In figure 15 you can also see on the right of the page range box is the option to print multiple copies of the web page.

Put it into practice:

Now let's put what we just learned into practice. The following is a list of exercises to do to help you print web pages from the Internet.

1. *Launch Internet Explorer*
2. *In the Address Bar, type Encarta.MSN.com. This brings up the MSN Encarta website.*
3. *In the Encarta search box type whale*
4. *Pull up the topic on Blue whales*
5. *Click on the find option*
6. *With the mouse, highlight the first sentence.*
7. *From the menu bar choose File then choose print.*
8. *On the print menu choose selection and click print. This will print the first sentence that you highlighted in step 6.*
9. *From the menu bar choose File and then choose print once more.*
10. *On the print menu type 1 under pages. This will print page 1.*

Making Information More Presentable

In this section we'll take a step further and copy text to other programs. We'll also save graphics file for use in other programs as well.

Concepts

Many times you want to use a selection from the Internet in another program. To do this we'll need to start by explaining a couple of concepts.

Copy and Paste

On a computer when you want to take information from one place to another it is called copying. You can copy information from one program to another or one place within a program to another place. For example we can copy information from a web page to a word processor.

We can also copy a paragraph within a word processor from one page to another. The process of doing this is called copy and paste. You would highlight what you want to copy, choose copy from a menu, go to where you want the copy to end up, and choose paste from a menu. We'll go into more detail in an example to follow.

Clipboard

There is a place in computers called the clipboard where the information is stored when we are using the copy command. It is like we place our selection on a cloud, then when we choose paste we get the information from the cloud and put it in the place we choose.

Saving

On some web pages you can save the web page or just a portion to a file. For example, if you like the picture of the blue whale on the Encarta web page you can save it. Below is an explanation of common file types and where they are used.

Text — These are files that can be pulled up in free programs. These programs, such as WordPad or notepad, come for free on the computer when you buy it. The ending of the files are .txt.

Image — These are files that are pulled up in graphic programs. There is a free graphic program that comes with computers called paint. Some of the ending of these files are .gif, .tif, jpg, bmp. The file types are different and some will work best with certain programs, while others work with all programs.

Other — Other programs have special endings. Microsoft programs are very common. The word processing program puts a .doc after the file name. Publisher, a fancier word processor puts a .pub after the file name. Many, many other programs name files special so they will open up automatically in their program. These special file names help computer users open files easily so we don't have to know what program the file was made in.

Copy and Paste Example

For our example we'll continue to use our Blue Whales article from the MSN Encarta web site. We'll also use a free program that comes on most computers. What we are going to do in our first example is copy some text from Internet Explorer to WordPad, the free word processor accessory that comes with Microsoft operating systems.

First we'll pull up Internet Explorer and get back to our Blue Whales article on MSN Encarta. Once we have pulled up our article we get to WordPad by going to the Start Menu, choosing All Programs, Accessories, and then clicking on WordPad. Whenever you have more than one program open they will line up at the bottom of the screen so you can easily move between them, as shown in Figure 16 below.

(Figure 16)

Back in Internet Explorer we will highlight our first paragraph in the find view. Then we want to use the right mouse button and click in the middle of our first paragraph. After we click, we can see in Figure 17 below, copy shows up on the menu. We want to use the left mouse button then to choose copy from the menu.

Blue Whale

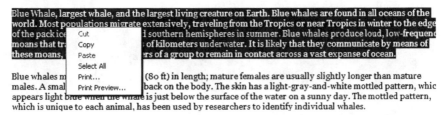

(Figure 17)

If you use a browser that doesn't have copy on that menu, you can find an Edit menu top of the browser screen. Copy will normally be listed under the Edit menu.

At this point, the selection we highlighted is now on the clipboard. We will now go to the bottom of the screen and choose WordPad to put our selection there. Once you click on WordPad you will have an empty document. You can use the right button to click and choose paste from the menu to put our selection into our WordPad document. Once we have done this we have successfully copied information from Internet Explorer into another program!

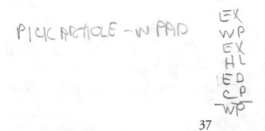

Put it into practice:

Now let's put what we just learned into practice. The following is a list of exercises to do to help you copy contents of web pages from the Internet.

1. *Launch Internet Explorer*
2. *In the Address Bar, type Encarta.MSN.com. This brings up the MSN Encarta website.*
3. *In the Encarta search box type whale*
4. *Pull up the topic on Blue whales*
5. *Click on the find option*
6. *On the Start Menu on the bottom of the screen, choose All Programs, then Accessories, then WordPad*
7. *At the bottom of the screen choose the Internet Explorer application that says Blue Whale – Search.... to get back to our blue whale article.*
8. *With the mouse, highlight the first paragraph.*
9. *While pointing in the middle of the highlighted paragraph, click the right mouse button.*
10. *Choose copy from the menu that comes up*
11. *At the bottom of the screen choose Document – WordPad to get back to our WordPad application.*
12. *With the mouse, click the right mouse button*
13. *Choose paste from the menu that comes up.*

Save Example

For our example we'll continue to use our Blue Whale article from the MSN Encarta web site. We'll also use a program that comes free on most computers. What we are going to do in our first example is save our blue whale picture and bring it up in a free graphics program that comes with Microsoft based computers.

First we'll pull up Internet Explorer and get back to our Blue Whales article on MSN Encarta. We'll click on the blue whale picture to pull it up. We can then point to the middle of the picture and we can use our right mouse button to bring up a menu. As shown on figure 18, the menu has a "Save Picture As" option on it

(Figure 18)

When we choose the Save as option from programs it will bring up the dialog box as shown in figure 19.

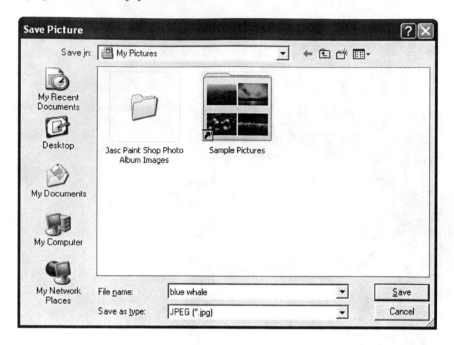

(Figure 19)

When we think about what we want to name things it is important we choose something that makes sense. In the bottom of the save box where it says "file name" we will name what we want to save. In this case let's name it blue whale. You can see that it will automatically add an ending. In this case it is a .jpg because our blue whale is a picture and .jpg is a graphic file type.

We will now pull up our blue whale picture that we saved in our free graphics program called "paint". We get to Paint by going to the Start Menu, choosing All Programs, Accessories, and then clicking on Paint. Just about all programs have a similar way of opening, saving and printing files. Once we are in Paint to pull up our file we will choose File from the menu at the top of the screen. We will then choose the open option from the file menu. This should bring up a box that lists perhaps many files, but should include our bluewhale.jpg file. You will click on that file name and choose open to see our picture.

Put it into practice:

Now let's put what we just learned into practice. The following is a list of exercises to do to help you save pictures from the Internet.

1. *Launch Internet Explorer*
2. *In the Address Bar, type Encarta.MSN.com. This brings up the MSN Encarta website.*
3. *In the Encarta search box type whale*
4. *Pull up the topic on Blue whales*
5. *Click on the Blue Whale picture*
6. *With the mouse, click on the right mouse button while on the picture.*
7. *From the menu, choose "Save file As"*
8. *In the box that comes up type blue whale in the filename box, then choose save.*
9. *On the Start Menu on the bottom of the screen, choose All Programs, then Accessories, then Paint*
10. *At the top menu, choose File, then choose Open*
11. *On the box that comes up pick the blue whale file and click open.*

<u>Chapter 4 -</u>
<u>Making Purchases on the</u>
<u>Internet</u>

There are a lot of things to buy on the Internet. Teens are most interested in buying music, cell phone ring tones, videos, and pictures on the Internet. Many things are nice to buy on the Internet but we need to be very careful. Teens need to be sure to first check with their parents before they tell anyone they will buy anything, especially on the Internet. In this chapter we will talk about how and where teens can safely buy items on the Internet.

Web Sites linked to electronic devices

Much of our population today owns one or more wireless electronic devices, such as a cellular phone, wireless organizers or pda's, or a wireless email device. These devices communicate via the Internet to many sites to download backgrounds, ring tones and other media such as video and songs. Even text messaging goes through the Internet to reach the other messaging devices we send to. This is something that happens in the background, with users of these devices simply unaware of what is happening. Is this dangerous? My opinion is no, it is just something to be aware of. However, in the hands of an uninformed person, this can lead to hidden costs depending on which plan the device's user is affiliated with.

We all hear nightmare stories of parents who get the $500.00 bill for the text messaging their teens did the first month they had their new cell phone. Depending on the plan, the charge usually appears on the monthly bill for the cell phone with no extra permission required than simply the use of the phone or wireless device. When setting up your ring tone most cell phones list "more ring tone options". This menu choice links to a special Internet site that the cell phone provider has setup for phones to connect to for downloading ring tones. These are generally safe sites, however parents should be aware of what teens are downloading as some music and ring tones could be inappropriate.

Safe methods to control costs and vulnerability

No matter if you are using one of the wireless devices above or a regular Internet portal on a computer to access a site on the Internet to purchase something, there are things you can do to control costs and limit the vulnerability you have to fraud and excessive charges.

- *There are phones and wireless device plans with limited capability and limited messaging and minutes on them.*
- *There are gift cards that you can buy from all of the major web sites that allow people to shop and only spend within the gift card limit.*
- *There are parental controls in software which limit which web sites can be accessed by users of computers.*
- *There are ways to program wireless devices where they can be deactivated upon being lost*

Email solicitations

Once you have purchased something on the Internet it is just about guaranteed that your email will fill with offers from the company you purchased from and any affiliate that they felt was worthy to know your email address. Much of this is called spam, which is a topic discussed in more detail in chapter 6. One caveat to purchasing on the Internet is that it will likely generate a lot of email because many companies use the email address of the purchaser as the login to make purchases. It's a buyer beware situation, so it's best to only buy from a few well known companies instead of buying from many lesser known companies.

Reputation

When it comes to buying things on the Internet, you need to ask someone about the reputation of the web site you want to buy from. As web sites become popular and are well used they get a good reputation. If they are not careful about their customers security or are careless with the information you give them they will get a bad reputation. On some websites they let the customers rank the store they are buying from. This is usually done in a 1 to 5 star system, where 5 stars means the store has been responsible in getting the purchased items to the customers.

Ease of Use

When using a website from a computer the ease of use of the website is another factor to consider, especially when considering letting teens purchase items. If a website has a lot of ads that are popping up on the screen, it is less likely to be safe. These pop-ups can actually cause hidden code to be installed and run on your computer. The pop-ups can also have undesirable material for teens that parents might not want them to see. When looking at web sites for ease of use factors consider:

- *Pop-ups or other advertising - The fewer pop-ups and ads, the better!*
- *Easy to find items - do you have to search the whole site to find what you want or are there categories and easy way to finds items especially interesting to teens?*
- *Easy checkout - what information do they require on checkout? Too much personal information is a bad thing.*
- *Do they provide and redeem gift certificates?*
- *Does the website seem secure according to the guidelines in the next section?*

How to tell a web site is safe to buy from

While there is no way to tell for sure that a site is safe to buy from, there are a few signs on your screen that will help you determine if the company tries to make it safe. When you go to a web site that is safe to purchase from, and you are ready to purchase the items you have selected, it will show you a lock on a part of the screen, as shown with the arrow in figure 20.

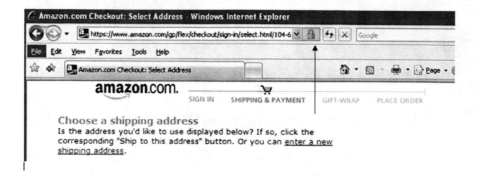

(Figure 20)

The lock indicates that the site uses certificates, which is a computer form of security. Let's go through a couple of definitions and concepts to help us understand certificates.

Certificates

A certificate is a file that is on our computer that someone gives us that is supposed to guarantee that doing business with them is safe. It gets on our computer through a process similar to a game of code words. In the game of code words two players make up a code word and its meaning. When they use that code word, even around their parents, only they know what they really mean. For instance they might say that the word grass means pet the dog. Then it will take a while for people to guess what the code word means until they pick up on the fact that the players pet the dog each time they use the word grass. During the certificate processes the computers make up and agree on a code word that no one else but the two computers know about. Then each time you visit a web site the computers tell each other the word again and so recognize that it's safe. Once they recognize its safe the lock will appear and so the computer user knows it's safe too. The companies we buy things from can only get these certificates by proving who they are and provide information about their honesty. When the companies have the certificates, over time it proves they can be trusted.

EV Certificate

An Extended Validation Certificate is a new version of certificate that also exchanges more information than before so the computer user can see more information about the company they are buying from.

Authentication

Authentication is a term that simply is the process that the computers use to verify that the certificate is good.

Encryption

Encryption is a term that describes how our information travels to a site that we are buying something from. It is like writing a note to a friend in code. Only you and the friend can decode the message, others must know the secret code to read the message. If a site uses encryption it scrambles the messages going between our computer and the web site so no one else can read what we're sending. This is very important if we are purchasing something using a credit card.

Colors on the Internet Explorer address bar

When the certificates or EV certificates are used the Internet Explorer address bar may change colors. If you go to a web site to buy something and the address bar turns green it is a good sign. This means the web site is using the EV certificates. If the address bar turns yellow or red you may not want to buy anything because the company isn't careful about the security they are using for their customers.

Put it into practice:

Now let's put what we just learned into practice. The following is a list of exercises to do to help you see if web pages are safe on the Internet. Please note you do not have to purchase anything to finish this exercise. I recommend you do this exercise with an adult or teacher to help you.

1. *Launch Internet Explorer*
2. *In the Address Bar, type www.randomhouse.com. This brings up a website where you can buy books for kids.*
3. *Click on the heading titled "kids".*
4. *Pick a book to purchase by clicking on it*
5. *Find the add to cart button and click it.*
6. *On the next screen click on begin check out*
7. *On the next screen click on begin check out again.*
8. *At this point you should see a lock at the top of the screen. Click on the lock and read the information.*
9. *Exit out of Internet Explorer.*

Example of purchasing on the Internet

I am going to use the Apple I-Tunes site as an example because it is a well established, safe way to purchase music from the Internet. There are competitors that have established safe ways as well; however this one is very popular and most likely to be used in conjunction with the music devices that are sold the most. I-Tunes is the software that is free and available from the Apple site that plays music, video and other media. It is also the store site provided by Apple to purchase music, videos, movies and other media. The site can be reached at http://www.apple.com/itunes. We'll look at the site based on the ease of use criteria we outlined earlier in the chapter.

As mentioned in the ease of use criteria, there is a spot on the ITunes website that allows you to buy and redeem gift cards, as shown in figure 21 below.

(Figure 21)

As shown below, the site is friendly and makes things easy to find.

(Figure 22)

The site does not have many pop-ups and does not display undesirable material on the main shopping pages. When an account is created there is very little personal information asked for. The main Apple website is secure and the items you buy through creating an account within the I-Tunes software is also transmitted securely as outlined in this chapter.

Put it into practice:

Now let's put what we just learned into practice. The following is a list of exercises to do to help you see the different music sites and gain insight from a parent on what they approve of.

1. *Launch Internet Explorer*
2. *In the Address Bar, type www.apple.com/itunes. This brings up a website where you can buy music.*
3. *Take a good look around the site*
4. *In the Address Bar, type http://www.zune.net/en-US/. This brings up a competing website where you can buy music.*
5. *Compare and contrast the site with a parent to gain their guidance in what music you should buy and how to buy it.*
6. *Exit out of Internet Explorer.*

Chapter 5 - Social Networking Sites - Examples and Tips

Social Networking Sites provide a wonderful outlet for both teens and adults while being at home or in another safe place. Social Networking Sites include chat rooms, dating sites, and other popular "friends meeting friends" sites like Facebook and MySpace. We have all heard both positive and negative information about these types of sites, and the purpose of this chapter is to highlight the positive and make teens and parents aware of the elements of each type of site that we want to be careful about.

Chat Rooms

Chat Rooms are basically sites that you can navigate where you can go into a "room", find out who else is there and strike up a conversation. The conversation is typed in real time - so you can see what people are typing as they type it. Each person is identified so you can see who is typing. The whole objective is to meet either those we know, or people we don't, and talk.

Safety Tips:

There are some specific tips we will want to discuss regarding chat rooms.

·   *Private vs. Public - Be aware of which chat rooms are private vs. public. Public chat rooms are where there are*

> many people gathered having conversations. This is safer
> because predators and other people who would try to
> have a questionable conversation are more accountable
> in public chat rooms. Sometimes in public chat rooms
> a person may invite another into a private room. It is
> important for teens and other children to not do this.
> It would be like going into a stranger's house without
> supervision - in other words, it's just not safe.

- *Check to see that the chat room is monitored. Monitored chat rooms have less of a chance for prolonged improper conversations to occur.*
- *Don't give out personal information. Choose a screen or login name that is gender neutral. Don't give out your real name.*
- *If someone says anything you are uncomfortable with make a note where you were, exit immediately and tell your parents.*

Dating Sites

Dating sites are specifically designed to meet strangers. There are more than 100 dating sites on the Internet. Some of them attempt to select people to meet based on the level of interest in other people, such as friendship, dating, or serious. There are some that have better ratings than others. Basic rules such as outlined above for chat rooms and in the next section regarding other social networking sites should be applied as well to dating sites, as they are really just specialized networking sites.

Other Social Networking Sites

There are lots of social networking sites, all of which have their positive side and their negative side. In this section we will take a glance at the main features of most social networking sites by looking at the web sites and registration screens for two of the most popular sites, those being MySpace and Facebook.

(Figure 23)

As seen above in figure 23, the MySpace website has many features including, movies, videos, chat rooms, books, IM (Instant Messaging), News, Ring tones and many others features. The signup page initially asks minimal information to start an account, after which the site assists you in setting up a profile that contains much more detailed information.

The website has extensive privacy policy and agreement screens you are recommended to read and you must check a box saying you have read and agree to the terms.

Facebook, which is another very popular social networking site, has similar features. Their approach to the initial page is different, as shown in the next screenshot. While MySpace chooses to advertise their features and offerings, Facebook chose a lower profile on their main page which really promotes the concept of encouraging membership and age appropriateness. While it does outline its features on the main page, the different style makes the page less crowded and shows less "advertisement-like" hype.

(Figure 24)

Facebook also has extensive privacy and policy statements for new registrants to read and adhere to. One of the features on the Facebook is extensive help and information about the site. This kind of information is helpful for a site to provide, so parents can determine if they want their teens to participate in the particular site.

The Facebook sign up page, as shown next in Figure 25, has some similarities to the MySpace sign up page, in that it is pretty simple and requires minimal information to establish the account. The Facebook sign up page does feature a security area where you have to type two words that are scrambled to complete the signup. This feature prevents people from creating a mass number of accounts without using their sign up page. Internet "hackers" or people that are meaning harm to a website could use an electronic technique of trying to add a mass number of accounts to cause the website to cease functioning for a period of time. Once someone has established an account, they go on to create an extensive profile.

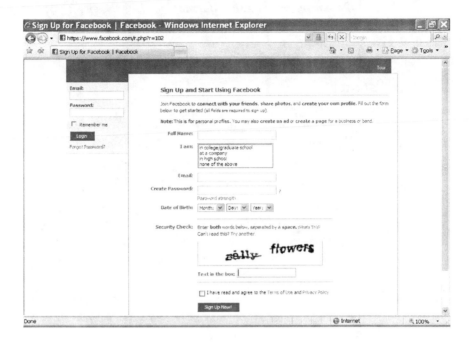

(Figure 25)

Tips

Related specifically to Social Networking sites, there are tips for parents as well as teens. For teens:

- *Make sure that your parents or guardians approve all sites before establishing accounts*
- *Share your profile information with your parents or guardians to make sure they approve of what you've entered into the screens*
- *Do not put too much personal information, leave optional fields blank*
- *Do not put pictures in the profile that suggest any affiliation with social groups or suggest social behavior.*

> *This can attract prejudice and predators, either of which would be unwelcome to your family.*

- *Do not share schedule information, like when you are due to go or come from home. This can leave your home vulnerable to theft.*

Tips For Parents:

- *Check out the sites your teen is joining. Several parents have gone to the length of joining as well and asking their teen to add them to their friends groups. This gives you access to the teens on-line chats and lets you see their profile.*
- *Don't be afraid to spy. Contrary to what your teen may say, children do need boundaries and guidance. They oftentimes push the borders of what you've told them just to make sure you still care for them.*
- *Make sure what your teen says or pictures they post won't attract a crowd you wouldn't have them around. It is important that you watch their on-line friends just like you would the other teens they bring to your house.*
- *Stay savvy on language nuances. The language that is used, whether on line or in person, has subtleties and hidden meanings.*
- *Put limits on time that your teen can be online. Just as in face to face meetings the online crowds can change depending on the time of day. If all of their friends have to be off-line at a certain time it's best to keep your teen off-line as well so they don't run into strangers you may not want them talking to.*

<u>Put it into practice:</u>

Now let's put what we just learned into practice. The following is a list of exercises to do with a parent to help you assist in discussing their guidelines regarding social networking sites.

1.   *Launch Internet Explorer*
2.   *In the Address Bar, type www.facebook.com. This brings up the facebook website.*
3.   *Take the site tour and discuss the various items that they outline in the profile. Discuss what your answers would be and see if your parent agrees with them.*
4.   *Read the privacy and guidelines or "etiquette" information for the site and discuss appropriate on-line behavior with your parent.*
5.   *Go to the myspace.com website and discuss the differences with your parent.*
6.   *Establish the rules for on-line activity with your parent, such as amount of time spent on the sites, which hours are available for surfing and which sites they want you to stay away from.*
7.   *Exit out of Internet Explorer.*

Chapter 6 - On-Line Predators and Safety Tips for Parents

The purpose of this chapter is to make both teens and parents aware of some of the things to watch out for while on the Internet interacting with other people. As much as we all hate to admit it, on-line predators are out there in every community and it is very important that we be aware and cautious. The purpose here is not to invoke fear or paranoia but give knowledge so teens can be smart in how they interact with others on the Internet. This chapter will outline what to watch for in regard to on-line predators as well as give tips to both teens and parents that will help avoid potentially dangerous situations for their families.

On-Line Predators - What to Watch For

Here's something to think about: It is interesting how just 20 years ago interacting on the Internet didn't really exist, especially the way it does today. Back then parents would tell their kids, "Don't talk to strangers". That meant that if someone you didn't know approached you, you would walk away without allowing that person to start a conversation with you. You could see the person, and perhaps even judge if you thought they were good or bad. You could tell their approximate age and if they meant you harm. What a contrast to the Internet! We can't see the person we correspond with. Therefore we can't tell what they look like, because they can send a false picture. We can't tell their approximate age because they could not be telling us the truth. We can't even really tell if they mean us harm. Kids today are still told "Don't talk to strangers", but does that apply to their Internet use? In this chapter we'll go over some guidelines for how to have fun but use caution when meeting new people on the Internet, the same way we use caution when we meet new people in person.

How Predators Work

By definition predators are people who seek out others to gain what they want without regard of the feelings of others. In gaining what they want, they can, and will, go as far as to harm others. Predators on the Internet are often disguised as someone who is friendly, outgoing, compassionate and willing to help kids.

Predators can contact kids in a variety of ways. They can use chat rooms, social networking sites, email, instant messaging and discussion sites. They are most often a part of a crowded site, one where many people gather and chat so they can blend in and search for possible vulnerable kids. As stated above they are often friendly, outgoing and can pose as the "new kid on the block" to get into conversations with strangers.

Predators often work toward either discussing inappropriate material with teens or try to arrange face to face meetings. Some start with inappropriate jokes to see if any of the teens seem to be attracted to such jokes. From the jokes they can graduate to other discussions, perhaps even asking the teen for personal information during the discussion. The predator will often ask for pictures, exchanging false, attractive looking photos if the teen seems willing to meet face to face. Sometimes the predator will offer pornography or other graphic movies or pictures to see how willing a teen is to participate in such activities. If the predator is working toward a face to face meeting or just wanting to gain personal access to the teen they may discuss the teens schedule with them. Many times they will ask about the family schedule to see when the teen may be left alone. Address information is often information that a predator is interested in to gain access to the teen in person as well. A predator could also be someone willing to steal from the teen or their family by gaining address and schedule information.

Safety Tips for Teens

Below is a bulleted list of things for teens to keep in mind while surfing the Internet.

- *When filling in registration forms for sites only fill in minimal information, avoiding putting personal information down*
- *Don't share your schedule or the schedule of anyone else in your family with someone you don't know.*
- *Don't send email or pictures to someone you have not met in person.*
- *Don't believe everything you read on the Internet, verify information before using it or repeating it.*
- *Visit with adults about friendships you make online.*
- *Tell your parents if someone says something online that makes you feel uncomfortable.*
- *Do not open an email from someone you don't know.*

Safety Tips for Parents

Keeping your computer safe helps keep you safe. All of the programs we discuss in this chapter either come with the computer or can be purchased for the computer. In either case, they are very important to have so they should be put on the computer before kids are allowed on the Internet.

Tips for Parents Regarding Teens and computer time

Regarding our teens there are specific things we need to do to keep them safe. Below is a bullet list of items that will help keep them safe and parents aware of what is going on with their teen:

- *Parents should become Internet knowledgeable. Don't just think the kids are the ones who "know it all". It is very important that parents know about the Internet in order for them to be able to discern when their child could be in trouble or being approached by a predator.*
- *Communicate, Communicate, Communicate. Even though many teens don't converse with parents as much as we'd like it is important that we talk to them about their online experiences. Talk about the online friends they've met, the type of people that are on various sites, what emails they've been getting, what sites they've found and what things they'd like to buy.*
- *Create house rules about surfing the Internet that are enforced. Things like the amount of time, Internet Sites that can be visited, amount of money spent are topics that are vital.*
- *Watch for changes in the teen. We all know that teens change based on the influence of those around them. It is very important to take the influences they receive from Internet friendships into consideration when evaluating behavior.*
- *Never put the computer in a teen's room. It should be in a public place to deter temptations of going to sites that would not usually be visited if someone was watching.*
- *Hold your teen accountable for online behavior, just as you would any public behavior. Things are often said bolder on-line due to not being able to see the other people they are talking to. It is important they follow rules established in chat rooms and use good etiquette.*

Safety Tips for using computers

Protection from Bad Email

You may have heard of the term Spam before. Spam is an email that is meant to get you to buy something you shouldn't. It may also ask you to give someone something you shouldn't. The companies that help us get our email have programs we can sign up for that help us not get as much spam. If you don't recognize who an email is from the rule is - Don't Open It! One of the terms that we will discuss in another section below is phishing. Phishing emails are emails that are "fishing around" for your private information. They are often tricky and make it seem like they would be real and important for you to answer their questions. Be suspicious of every email from a company, because it could not be real if they are asking personal questions.

Protection from Intruders

Just like we lock our doors at night, we need to put some locks on our computers so we don't let bad people into them. We do this by having something called a "firewall" which helps protect us from traffic that is known for bad things. It's like if someone knocked on your door wearing a mask, and you didn't recognize them, you wouldn't open the door. Firewalls look for masks and other signs that the stuff trying to get into your computer could be bad.

Protection from Bad Programs

There are people who write bad programs that can damage or steal information from your computer. Bad programs are actually called many things. They can be called a virus or spyware, or botware. We'll discuss each type in this section.

Viruses are programs that generally do damage to your computer. Anti-Virus Software keeps bad programs that are meant to do our computer harm from getting on our computer by acting like a shield when programs try to get in. Anti-Virus Software also scans your computer every once in a while to make sure no virus was sneaky enough to get through its shield.

Spyware is a program that acts like a spy on your computer, seeing what information it can gather and report back to whoever sent it. Many times spyware programs are meant to gather personal information such as credit card information, so thieves can steal from you. Anti-Spyware programs work like Anti-Virus programs to give you a shield when the programs try to get in and do a scan.

Botware is a program that is used to remotely assist someone that is sending out spam. There are people who write programs to send out spam. If a botware program gets on your computer then your computer will be sending out spam without you knowing about it. Most Anti-Virus and Anti-Spyware programs help keep these off our computers.

Protection from Bad Web Sites

It isn't always easy to tell if a web site may have something bad on it. Many times the web site might look just fine then something will "pop up" on the screen. These may be advertisements or just pictures that aren't good for teen's eyes to see. There is software called "pop up blockers" that block the pop ups. Some sites also gather innocent information from you, such as your email address just so they can include you in junk or Phising email as I mentioned in the bad email section above.

Features of Internet Explorer

The latest version of many browsers has some of the features I mentioned above. In this section we will cover the specific features of Internet Explorer 7. Internet Explorer 7 has pop up blockers and Anti-Phishing tools. The pop up blocker comes up at the top of the screen when you go to a site that uses pop ups. Many popular sites sell ads to support their site, and many of the ads come in the form of pop-ups. The screen says the pop up is blocked and it also shows the options once you click on the blocking bar. You can temporarily allow pop-ups from this web page, always allow them, or go into the settings area and turn off the blocker completely.

There are two items that are noticeable in the Internet Explorer status bar which is the bar at the bottom of the Internet Explorer screen. The left most icon shows when there are pop-ups being blocked. The right icon, also shown with an exclamation point, displays when a site is being checked for being a phishing site. If the website is a phishing site, and as long the phishing filter is on, Internet Explorer will bring up a web page that tells you that the site is a phishing site and give directions on what to do.

Internet Filters

An additional item that is very important to have on the computer is an Internet filter. Many of the filters are free; some you must pay a fee for. These filters block inappropriate sites based on rules that are set up by teachers or parents. If a child happens upon an inappropriate site another screen will pop up with a message and block the access to that site completely.

Examples of programs for PopUps, Phishing, Viruses, Spyware and Firewalls

As I mentioned above, Internet Explorer has some built in tools to help prevent PopUps and show which web sites are Phishing sites. There are also other tools you can buy that help in these areas as well. Ad-Aware is one example. Some other Internet browsers help in these areas too.

There is some software available that works for Viruses, Spyware and act as firewalls. Two of the biggest brands of these kinds of products are McAfee and Norton. These programs are not free but provide a good amount of protection. There is free software available, and most of it comes separately instead of working all together like the ones I just mentioned.

Viruses are prevented by antivirus software, and as I mentioned McAfee and Norton come with computers when you purchase them. Then after 90 days or so they will ask you to pay for a year or so to keep the software current. Totally free versions of software are available, but they don't always have all of the features you need, so take a good look before you get one.

Spyware is prevented by anti-spyware software. Many of the same rules as I mentioned for Virus software apply. Many of the same people that make antivirus software make anti-spyware software too. It is helpful to buy both of these programs from the same people so if you have problems you can call one place to get help.

Firewalls are made by many of the same vendors as the Antivirus and Anti-Spyware software that I mentioned above. There is also another popular Firewall called Zone Alarm that many people use. Some of the equipment that helps you get onto the Internet also come with a Firewall for free.

Must do's

In order to keep your computer safe here is a list of must do's.

- *Do buy or get free Antivirus Software.*
- *Do make sure your computer checks for updates to the Antivirus software at least daily.*
- *Do buy or get free Anti-Spyware Software*
- *Do make sure your Internet browser has a pop-up blocker and anti-phising tools built in and that they are on.*
- *Do buy or get a free Firewall. Have someone who knows about Firewalls help you configure it.*

Chapter 7 - Projects

This chapter provides two more projects to do to bring all of our concepts together. The projects will both involve looking up information, copying that information to another program and printing the information for review by an adult.

Project 1

For this project we want to look up information on internet predators with a parent.

1. *Launch Internet Explorer*
2. *In the search box, type internet predator*
3. *Analyze the results with your parent, reading at least 3 articles.*
4. *Write down the dangers you discover of Internet predators*
5. *Establish guidelines with your parent of where you will go on the Internet and how to react to inappropriate behavior by others on websites.*
6. *Look up the MSNBC series Dateline: To catch a Predator. Read the articles and discuss with a parent.*
7. *Exit the browser.*

Project 2

For this project we want to look up information on our favorite animal. We will copy the information and a picture of the flag to WordPad. We will finally print the information.

1. *Launch Internet Explorer*
2. *In the Address Bar, type Encarta.MSN.com.*
3. *In the search box type the name of your favorite animal and click search*
4. *Choose an article that looks like it gives good information and a picture of your favorite animal.*
5. *Highlight 2 paragraphs of information on the screen.*
6. *From the edit menu choose copy*
7. *Bring up the accessory WordPad from the start button, programs, accessories menu*
8. *From the edit menu choose paste*
9. *Return to the Internet browser by clicking on it on the task bar at the bottom of your screen.*
10. *Now click on the picture of your favorite animal and choose copy from the edit menu*
11. *Return to WordPad by clicking on it on the task bar at the bottom of your screen*
12. *Make sure you are at the bottom of the document you pasted in before and hit the Enter key on the keyboard to get to a new line.*
13. *Choose Paste from your edit menu to paste in the picture of the animal.*
14. *Hit the Enter key on the keyboard to get to a new line after the picture of the animal. Type in a nice sentence about the animal.*
15. *Choose save from the file menu and save your work under the name of your animal.*
16. *Choose print from the file menu and print your work.*

4 HP

4 8-50

33 37

LaVergne, TN USA
19 March 2010
176490LV00001B/89/P